John Uri Lloyd

The right Side of the Car

John Uri Lloyd

The right Side of the Car

ISBN/EAN: 9783337059491

Printed in Europe, USA, Canada, Australia, Japan

Cover: Foto ©ninafisch / pixelio.de

More available books at **www.hansebooks.com**

THE RIGHT SIDE OF THE CAR

BY

THE AUTHOR OF ETIDORHPA

(JOHN URI LLOYD)

DE ARTE ET VERITATE

BOSTON

RICHARD G. BADGER & COMPANY

M DCCC XCVII

TO MY WIFE

The illustrations are by Mr. J. Augustus Knapp; the cover design by Mr. Theodore Brown Hapgood, Jr.

List of Illustrations

Preface.

THIS sketch, designed as a slight tribute to womanhood, was written for one who takes on herself many cares that the author's shoulders should bear, and whose full praises can be sung only when words as yet unframed are put in print.

Fashioned for her alone, it came through accident before others, and in momentary indiscretion was read to the Cincinnati Woman's Club. Let him hope that in dress, at least, it may credit those who honored him by listening on that occasion, and who, indeed, are somewhat responsible for its present publication.

Yet the author seeks not to evade the blame, if any such be attached to this desire to please his friends. He must, perhaps, seek forgiveness from her who sat in the sunlight, who unconsciously inspired these lines, and who, now looking upward, sees always before her glad eyes those snow-capped scenes in the lovely land of the Sierras before whose beauty imagination pales.

Would that her face, which the author dare not venture to picture, might grace these pages; but it must remain unseen. Let the story of contrasts that spelled this pen suggest the vision that vanished in the sunshine of a lost summer.

Should this offering to innocence and purity, this token to the maiden and the wife, leave the reader craving yet another sentence, seeking yet another thought-step upward, the aim of the author will have been accomplished.

J. U. L.

The
Right Side of the Car.[1]

꭫

BY good fortune I had
been invited to ac-
company a person-
ally conducted
excursion party of
physicians, happy
mortals who, with
their wives as companions, gladly
looked forward to the pleasure of a
trip across the continent in a special
car. I was the only man among them
who was not a physician, and, after
having accepted their generous in-
vitation, I alone of all that happy
party looked backward. Homesick

---

[1] A story of the Northern Pacific Railway.

before the first wheel turned, the
" blues " possessed me entirely by
the end of the first hour ; and, dom-
inated by disagreeable thoughts, I
threw myself into a corner of the
parlor section, where, with a copy of
Solomon's proverbs, as best fitted to
my unsociable temperament, I was
left alone by my considerate friends.
Naturally, under the circumstances,
meditation and seclusion made me
sulkier still.

In the course of our journey a
telegram was brought to our director.
It came from a physician who, know-
ing of our excursion, asked if we
would escort a Miss Myrtle to her
home on the western coast, a request
which was willingly granted. The
ladies of our party playfully decided
that, since I travelled alone, it should
be my duty to serve as the young

"I returned to my brooding, a prey to
abnormal reflections."

girl's special attendant. This func-
tion I did not decline, though in
truth, I was too absent-minded to
take much interest in the matter,
or even to notice the good-natured
remarks of my fellow tourists. I
returned to my brooding, a prey to
abnormal reflections.

When I arose late the following
morning and parted the curtains in
front of my berth, I caught a glimpse
of a feminine outline in the section
opposite mine, and at once it flashed
upon me that here was the charge I
had almost unconsciously accepted.
Somewhat vexed, I glanced indiffer-
ently at the face of the girl who had
come to disturb my thoughts, when
suddenly my unconcern gave way to
curiosity. Her countenance was of
that peculiar cast which only once
or twice in a lifetime surprises one's

vision, telling as it does of experience, of soul development and intellectual attainment, though not of years. She may have been under fifteen, she may have been over twenty. Her full countenance was turned away, but even from the profile view I saw enough to enable me to guess of her past and to read something of her future. The maiden was surely treading rapidly the path that leads to silence. Although I sat out of the range of her vision, my steady, earnest gaze drew the girl's attention; for a moment she glanced at me, smiled pleasantly, and then turned back again, looking diagonally through the window into the northwest. That sudden faceflash was to my gloom as the glitter of a mirror that reflects into a shadowed crevice or deep grotto a sliver

32

of sunshine which could never have fallen directly into its depths. The girl's native gladness, expressed in a single kindly glance, had soothed my heart-throbs. Silently I thanked her — I, who a moment before considered her presence an infliction.

As the hours of that day passed, my accidental ward sat strangely absorbed in reverie, gazing ever into the northwest, and scarcely turning her head towards the others in the car. Even when addressed by one or another she answered dreamily, and seemed to be indifferent to their presence. It was saddening to see one so young and so fair thus closeting herself in unapproachable privacy, — a privilege, we are wont to think, of those whom age or long experience of sorrow consign to pessimistic gloom. The noisy party

3   33

surrounding us, revelling in mirth, did not interrupt this strange child's reverie, nor, indeed, did they disturb me; insensible to their happiness and to the varying charms of the flying landscape, I sat moodily in my own section. At last, by common consent, we two were left unheeded, — she alone in her sweetness, I in my acidity; but it made me glad to be in the car with this bright face.

Late in the afternoon the declining sun shone fiercely into that opposite section of the car; it was reflected with double heat across the arid plains that edge the great desert. Leaning towards the pale, listless maiden, I ventured to address her. " Will you not sit on the shady side of the car ? "

She turned her face to me and

34

answered, " I do not dislike the sun-shine. This is the right side of the car for me." Then she turned again towards the northwest, and in the full glare of the sun continued gaz-ing into the distance.

An annoying titter from some one who had observed my attempted advances reached my ear; by her it was unnoticed.

A waggish friend leaned over and whispered, " How is your charge ? "

" Do not disturb me," I replied. " Can you not see that this girl is not of your merry party, and that I am an unsocial guest? Leave me to myself, and do not annoy the girl." After this uncalled-for, petulant rebuke, I slunk back to the hermitage of my window-cur-tained alcove with freshly homesick feelings.

I sat in the shade, penetrated by the shadows, while on the other side of the car, saturated with brightness, unconscious of her beauty as is the drooping lily-of-the-valley, the girl shone in the sunlight. I watched her as a crusty botanist might study the charms of a morning-glory shrinking in the zenith of its loveliness. Would that I could describe her face! She was not what men call beautiful, yet the features were of extreme delicacy and refinement. The thin lips of wax-like translucence, the flushed cheek with its central spot, seemingly of artificial crimson, the great eyes so touchingly attractive, — all helped to tell the story of a life worn prematurely near to its close, of an unsullied soul stepping out of earth-light into God-light.

"Saturated with brightness, unconscious of
her beauty as is the drooping lily-of-the-valley,
the girl shone in the sunlight."

I sat in the shade, penetrated by the shadows, while on the other side of the car, saturated with brightness, unconscious of her beauty as is the drooping lily-of-the-valley, the girl shone in the sunlight. I watched her as a crusty botanist might study the charms of a morning-glory shrinking in the zenith of its loveliness. Would that I could describe her face! She was not what men call beautiful, yet the features were of extreme delicacy and refinement. The thin lips of wax-like translucence, the flushed cheek with its central spot, seemingly of artificial crimson, the great eyes so touchingly attractive, — all helped to tell the story of a life worn prematurely near to its close, of an unsullied soul stepping out of earth-light into God-light.

" Saturated with brightness, unconscious of her beauty as is the drooping lily-of-the-valley, the girl shone in the sunlight."

As an earth-born orchid is not earth-bound, but sends its feeler into space above; so this human creature of mortal mould, feebly clinging to things below, appeared to be reaching up into ethereal realms.

An indescribable sensation of mingled joy and sorrow came over me as I watched the peaceful face of the young girl, and thought how unconsciously she was standing at the very edge of eternity. In this mood the shadows of night found me, still wrapped in gloom, yet vaguely happy. On the maiden's brow I saw fall the last ray of the sun, but not the darkling shadows; for before the sunbeam vanished I averted my eyes.

When, next morning, I parted the curtains of my berth, I beheld the trim, girlish figure seated as before in the opposite section of the coach. I observed also that the serene face was still turned intently towards the northwest. Before going to breakfast, I stepped to her side, and said, " May I escort you to the dining-car ? "

" Thank you, I breakfasted at the first call," was the reply.

" Then I will offer to attend you to lunch when the noon hour comes. You have been placed in my charge, and," I added apologetically, " I am old enough to be your father."

" With pleasure," she answered, and I threw a triumphant look at my teasing fellow-travellers.

The day passed like the day before, — the fair invalid silent in her place, I morose in mine. Like a crab peeping from beneath a stone at a butterfly resting in the sunshine, I gazed at her who gave no heed to any one. With book neglected at her side, and lost in her meditations, she peered unceasingly through the window.

When in the afternoon the sun again shone upon her, I once more offered my place on the shady side, and she replied as before: " Thanks, but this is the right side of the car for me."

We had long since passed the Minnesota and eastern Dakota fields and meadows ; we had swept through the grotesque Bad-Lands of western Dakota, and crept over the arid plains beyond. We had moved up the picturesque valley of the Yellowstone, where for three hundred miles, valley, river, and hill form the most enchanting scenes. Day and night

came and went; we passed moun-
tain-gulches and canyons, rivers,
plains and mountains, to shoot at
last into the great fierce desert of
desolation that separates the Cascade
Range from the Rocky chain. One
of my companions finally ventured
to address me again concerning the
girl who sat opposite.

" For what is your charge looking ? "

" Be quiet," I whispered. " Can't
you see that she is leaning over the
verge of eternity and looking into
Heaven ? " I felt the bitterness of
my speech soon enough to arrest
my voice, and thus the finishing
sentence — " Neither you nor I
know what such as she can see " —
was unspoken.

But the question nettled me.
Why should not I, in whose charge

the girl had been placed, be told the reason of that persistent skyward gaze? With this thought in mind, I moved over to the seat beside her — an act which I had not presumed to venture on before — and abruptly said : —

" Tell me why you gaze so steadily through the window."

" I am looking for my home."

Her quick answer chimed so unexpectedly with the rhythm of my thoughts as to startle me. Did she realize that her fatal disease would soon take her to another home? And was she really looking into *its* windows?

" But we have travelled more than a thousand miles since you commenced your curious watch. How can you see your home through mountain-chains and sandhills, from the bottom of canyons and the winding bed of rivers, through desert dust-clouds that cover the way and blot out the landscape ? "

" Ah," she said, " I think of my home at times like these, and am looking for it now. I live at the base of Mount Tacoma."

" Mount Rainier, you mean," I interrupted.

" No, *not* Rainier ; " and as she spoke these words she flushed, and turned upon me a look of reproach. " Do you not love your own country ? " she continued. " Why do you call that noble mountain, ' the mother of mountains,' after an obscure British admiral who never saw this continent ? Shame on such Americans ! I look for Tacoma. That is the real name, the Indian

46

name given to the mountain long
before the British landed in America.
Tacoma, Mount Tacoma, my Tacoma!" The momentary flush
vanished, the pensive gaze returned;
her last words were uttered in a
plaintive, caressing tone. She continued softly : —

"I live near that noblest peak of
all the Cascade range, and I long
again to see it looming above my
home."

My question had touched and
opened her heart, yet after a slight
pause, as if to excuse herself for
withdrawing from conversation, she
said, "I am looking for my home
now," and again she turned her face
northwestward.

"But," I persisted, "we are in a
blinding desert. We must travel
three hundred miles before you

reach your mountain. Would it not be better for you to join our party, to talk and laugh with the young people, instead of sitting lonely here?"

"Ah," she replied, ignoring my suggestion, her mind dwelling only on her beloved mountain, — "three hundred miles, did you say? Then I am very near the end of my journey. You do not know Tacoma, else you would not speak so lightly. Only three hundred miles from my home!" And once more she turned to the northwest.

"May I stay here beside you?" I asked, then impulsively added: "You are in the sunlight, I am in the shadow. Your home is before you, your thoughts are happy, your hopes are radiant; my home lies far behind, and to me the shadows ever

48

lengthen. May I sit here in the sunlight with you?"

"Yes," she replied, but, unconscious of the bitterness covered by my words, she gave me no glance.

And so, side by side, we passed into the depths of that dreariest of American deserts, all sage brush and prickly pear, sand and heat; until at last even the contorted sage brush disappeared, the splotches of cactus vanished; we had passed nature's life-line. No vegetation could thrive in that torrid earth; only white sand and white heat remained.

Then, as by a wizard's touch, my mind closed to things about and to scenes behind; the great desert disappeared; the white-hot sun dimmed; the voices of my companions were silenced; the rattling

4   49

wheels and the puffing of the engine were unheard; the thumping of the anguished heart that never stops writhing in pain, that cries unceasingly, " Do not forget, do not forget," was at last forgotten. Things material had passed away, and, neither awake nor asleep, I sat beside the unsociable girl, she gazing into the depths of space through one pane of glass, I staring through another. At last, at last in life's journey, I rested on the right side of the car.

How long this exalted mental state continued I know not. But when normal consciousness returned I saw before my eyes on the distant horizon's edge, a strange dome-shaped, cloud-like something that I felt was not a cloud, because it was less substantial even than a bank of

"I saw before my eyes, on the distant horizon's edge, a curious dome-shaped, cloud-like something that I felt was not a cloud, because it was less substantial even than a bank of mist."

wheels and the puffing of the engine were unheard; the thumping of the anguished heart that never stops writhing in pain, that cries unceasingly, " Do not forget, do not forget," was at last forgotten. Things material had passed away, and, neither awake nor asleep, I sat beside the unsociable girl, she gazing into the depths of space through one pane of glass, I staring through another. At last, at last in life's journey, I rested on the right side of the car.

How long this exalted mental state continued I know not. But when normal consciousness returned I saw before my eyes on the distant horizon's edge, a strange dome-shaped, cloud-like something that I felt was not a cloud, because it was less substantial even than a bank of

" I saw before my eyes, on the distant horizon's edge, a curious dome-shaped, cloud-like something that I felt was not a cloud, because it was less substantial even than a bank of mist."

mist. It seemed as if God, having fashioned a crystal icicle, had tipped it with a drift of purest snow, and with this pencil had outlined a gigantic cone on the white sky, its base resting on the horizon.

But this was not all. It seemed as if the great I AM had then grasped the sun's rays, and sweeping them into glistening strands had spun a web finer than gossamer, shading the silver film with golden beams of pure moonlight, and had thrown this wondrous fabric over the mighty arch, enveloping it from cone-tip to horizon-base.

The heavens above were white, the sand below was white, and the enchanting sky-tracing was also white. White showed upon white, and white was between ; three whites in one, and each distinct.

Heaven's "huge rondure" flashed with sunshine. The great plain about, from centre to circumference, spread dazzling in the sunshine, and that wondrous spectacle afar, the only object to break the circle that told where sky and desert met, stood, phantom-like, the very spirit of purity, in the sunshine. This dazzling marvel was less than cloud; it appeared non-material; I felt that a breath of air might have swept it into space, only there was not motion enough in that glittering desert to move a phantom. Had a silver cloud risen behind the heavenly spectre, its filmy outline would have shone through the ethereal creation that was seemingly intermediate between imagination and matter.

Enraptured, I turned to the girl

beside me, who, with the window-frame between herself and the sky-cone, could not perceive it.

" Look," I said. " See the marvellous wonder-cloud that has risen above the horizon."

She leaned towards me, — even against me, — and shot a quick glance through my window-pane.

"Tacoma! Tacoma!" cried the girl. " At last, at last, my beloved Tacoma ! "

She clasped her hands, her face uplifted, and as tears of joy fell from her eyes, she murmured softly (only I could hear that whisper), " Tacoma, I'm coming! — I'm coming !"

The hands relaxed, the eyes closed peacefully, as when a weary babe sleeps ; her head drooped and rested gently on my shoulder ; I sat alone, — all alone in that seat on the right side of the car.

. . . . . .

Never before nor after could that lovely girl have loosened life's thread so gracefully. Never before nor after could that pure spirit have gone into the colorless beyond so peacefully. Never before could that life-page have been folded in such purity on earth, and never after could it have been opened in such loveliness in heaven.

The ice on Tacoma's frozen slopes is not different from other ice-cliffs; the upheaved volcanic formation beneath this frigid cloak is only rock. Not for these do I love Tacoma, but for the sake of the strange girl whose memory is sacred, of her for whom

Mt. Tacoma stands a crystal monument.

God grant that when at last I see the sky-tracings that speak of my Tacoma, I may again be on the " Right Side of the Car."

FINIS

PRINTED BY JOHN WILSON AND SON
AT THE UNIVERSITY PRESS, CAM-
BRIDGE, FOR RICHARD G. BADGER
AND COMPANY, PUBLISHERS, BOSTON

ETIDORHPA;

OR,

THE END OF EARTH.

By JOHN URI LLOYD.

With many Illustrations.

Eighth Edition.

Deeply spiritual — a literary masterpiece and a prophecy of development. — *The Arena.*

Profoundly scientific. — *The American Druggist.*

Thoughtful, occult, and distinctly novel. — *New York World.*

Widely read and highly praised. — *Hartford Post.*

8vo, cloth. By mail, prepaid, for $2.00.

THE ROBERT CLARKE CO.

Publishers, Cincinnati.

Mailed by RICHARD G. BADGER & Co., Boston, at publishers' price.

Messrs. R. G. BADGER & COMPANY take pleasure in announcing the following volume as in rapid preparation.

THE CHILDREN OF THE NIGHT.
By EDWIN ARLINGTON ROBINSON. With specially designed covers. Printed on antique wove paper at the University Press. 16mo, about 150 pp. $1.25 *net*.

Also fifty copies on Imperial Japanese vellum, $3.00 *net*.

Speaking of a small, privately printed volume of Mr. Robinson's poems, issued some time since, "The Bookman" says: "There is true fire in his verse, and there are the swing and the singing of the winds and waves and the passion of human emotions in his lines, — here and there in a sonnet the cry of a yearning spirit enters the lute of Orpheus and sounds a sweet and wondrous note."

This same little volume was spoken of in "The Outlook" by Mr. Edward Eggleston as "a book that I cannot help reading;" and Miss Helen A. Clarke, in her editorial criticisms in "Poet-lore," says: "His verse has more power to hold the attention than anything we have seen lately."

The present volume is in reality Mr. Robinson's first published work, the volume which created these comments being a small, privately printed pamphlet, entitled "The Torrent and the Night Before," now absolutely unobtainable. "The Children of the Night" includes the best of those poems that appeared in the earlier volume, and contains, in addition, much work that has never before been published.

THE LITERARY REVIEW.
A Monthly News Journal of Belles Lettres.

It is the aim of the publishers to give the selected news of the literary world in a concise, readable form, and to present in the contributed articles such material as is most likely to interest the makers and the readers of books.

Its contents consists of original Essays, Stories, and Verse ; a department of Correspondence ; a department styled The Reviewer's Notes, made up of such matter as this heading would indicate ; a department of Markings from Books, being the most brilliant sayings from the newest books, and Reviews of all the important Publications. These reviews are both serious and entertaining, which is, the publishers believe, a somewhat startling innovation. From time to time are issued special numbers containing a larger amount of fiction, and giving in addition carefully executed art supplements of the highest merit.

On the score of literary as well as typographical excellence the publishers invite comparison with any other publication of its class.

The publishers, moreover, do not stand alone in this opinion. Says the "Boston Beacon" : "The Literary Review deserves the attention of readers of current literature. It is a well-edited and handsomely printed journal, and numbers experienced writers among its contributors." It is the opinion of "The Inland Printer" that "The Literary Review makes up in brightness for its lack in years," and the same magazine thinks "the reviewer's columns are extraordinarily spicy."

Single copy, 5 cents. Yearly subscription, 50 cents.

PUBLISHED BY

RICHARD G. BADGER & COMPANY,
Boston.